Hunting Down the Monk

Hunting Down the Monk

❧

Poems by
Adrie Kusserow

Foreword by
Karen Swenson

BOA Editions, Ltd. ❧ Rochester, NY ❧ 2002

Publications by BOA Editions, Ltd.—
a not-for-profit corporation under section 501 (c) (3)
of the United States Internal Revenue Code—
are made possible with the assistance of grants from
the Literature Program of the New York State Council on the Arts,
the Literature Program of the National Endowment for the Arts,
the Sonia Raiziss Giop Charitable Foundation,
the Lannan Foundation,
as well as from the Mary S. Mulligan Charitable Trust,
the County of Monroe, NY,
Ames-Amzalak Memorial Trust,
and The CIRE Foundation.

See page 104 for special individual acknowledgments.

Cover Design: Daphne Poulin-Stofer
Cover Photo: "Woman's Work" by Robert Gorski, courtesy of the photographer
Interior Design and Typesetting: Richard Foerster

BOA Logo: Mirko

LIBRARY OF CONGRESS CATALOGING-IN-PUBLICATION DATA

Kusserow, Adrie.
  Hunting down the monk : poems / by Adrie Kusserow ; foreword by Karen
Swenson.
    p. cm. — (A. Poulin, Jr. new poets of America series ; v. 24)
  ISBN 1-929918-23-2
  I. Title. II. Series.

PS3611.U74 H86 2002
811'.6—dc21
                                                          2002027809

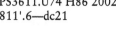

NATIONAL
ENDOWMENT
FOR THE ARTS

NYSCA

BOA Editions, Ltd.
Nora A. Jones, Executive Director/Publisher
Thom Ward, Editor/Production
Peter Conners, Editor/Marketing
Glenn William, BOA Board Chair
A. Poulin, Jr., President & Founder (1938 - 1996)
250 North Goodman Street, Suite 306
Rochester, NY 14607
www.boaeditions.org

For my mother, Suzanne Kusserow,
and for my father,
Berthold Karl Otto Kusserow, 1932–1975,
and for Robert Jan Lair

CONTENTS

———

FOREWORD

The Dalai Lama, characterizing Westerners who move, as Captain Sir Richard Burton did a century ago, from religion to religion in a quest for spiritual comfort, has called them/us "spiritual tourists." Burton moved from an arid Anglicanism, to Hinduism, to join an abstruse Moslem sect. The inheritors of his search have moved even farther afield. We are, a century after the advent of Darwin and more than a century after having embraced the scientific method, in the turmoil of a spiritual revolution, attempting to remake our understanding of religious and spiritual life. There is nothing we won't investigate, taste, smell, eat, or listen to in our search.

Adrie Kusserow in the poems of her starkly frank, frequently gritty first book confronts this situation like a boxer squaring off for a knockout. In the title poem, "Hunting Down the Monk" the nomads "wander from meaning station / to meaning station" looking for gods who "surface because / we feed them." This interdependence of god and humanity is a recurrent motif. Although the first poems are situated in Nepal she covers most, if not all, religious bases unstintingly—Unitarian, Jehovah's Witness, Greek Orthodox, snake-handling Christians and Buddhism, to name a few.

As is true of all exceptional poets, Kusserow not only isolates a painful conundrum of her time but imbues it with the emotional ambiance that reverberates about it, developing a depth of field around her subjects. The searchers in her poems may sometimes look foolish, but their pain and need is made searingly real to us. They are in crisis. The misunderstandings between the seekers and those who appear to be comfortably ensconced in their beliefs only intensify need and pain. The overwhelming desire to believe is a hunger, an anorexia, which she parallels hauntingly with the physical neediness of the East—hungry, desperate children, women unwittingly lured into prostitution in order to help their families eat. But Kusserow's universe is a difficult one full of questions, devoid of "cheap, creamy answers" even when what is being presented is "only God's words, / the whole truth, no additives."

Having been trained in a number of schools which will not allow her to pass easily through the eye of faith's needle, Kusserow is frustrated in her search. The Western disbelief in hierarchy, which as Solzhenitsyn has pointed out, automatically destroys moral authority, is a natural outcome of democracy and withers the ability to believe. Her rigorous training in the scientific method, as a cultural anthropologist, naturally casts out other beliefs because its god is doubt. She is caught, "hanging like a bat in the walls of the bardo" between her childhood Christ, a rainbow of religions, and science. A subsidiary problem is that all of these religions issue from men and tend to deny the rich sensuality of life. That sensuality is apparent in her lustrous use of the language she refuses to abrogate.

All of this, which could be a heavy, indeed, logy philosophical brew is rendered sharp, razor clean and clear as Himalayan air by her imagery and brilliant sense of words. She makes them crackle like morning frost on a tent at 16,000 feet. She creates not only her situations but her language new. The women of Kathmandu are "dressed like tropical drinks." Kathmandu itself is a "Buddhist base camp" full of "nouveau monks—in their Ray-Bans, Nikes, burgundy hair." Around all this she skulks like a dog to "sniff the borders / of other faiths." She is well aware that she is close to being like a woman who "shifts from red to chameleon lime depending / on what branch of God she's on." Returning to Protestantism in her mother's New England church she has a respite but no answer among "acres of elderly widows wearing gardens of pastels."

There is an umbilical cord for Kusserow between lack of belief and isolation, the desperate, if not despairing, loneliness with which all thinking Westerners are well acquainted. To not have a belief, a faith, is to be without community, to live your life as a singular entity, as a spider devoid of its web. Love and the sensual, birth and the relationship with both humans and nature provides the gifts of continuity and wholeness. Out of her sense of the sensual comes another sort of belief, a variety of pantheistic wonder that gives a spiritual connection with the world in her poem "Snowflake Bentley" about the man who first took photographs of snowflakes through a microscope. She describes how he sorted "snowflakes with a feather, / holding his breath / to spare the life of each flake" sensing, as she does herself,

> the snow crunching
> as his center of gravity slowly shifted,
> making room
> for the joy of the infinite
> opening inside him.

Kinship with both the human and natural world is what drives out isolation and creates community. We see this in Kusserow's response to the birth of her child, about which she has created a lovely, long lyrical poem. The child's newborn hunger echoes all the other hungers which have preceded her birth:

> Still nursing, but stormily now, legs kicking,
> her free hand batting against my chest
> like a small twig against a window.

Perhaps it is the giving to hunger rather than hungering that eases the ache around the vacancy where belief used to be.

Another replacement for Kusserow's faith is to love not the belief created by men but an individual man. The old yearning still lingers, however, as when she writes of "the way stained glass / renews a stale God." Through these various channels she arrives at an acceptance of death as an opening, which occurs when the body

> accepts
> what it fears:
> it moves from solid to liquid,
> it gives in and becomes the world.

The final poems in the book give evolution a spiritual rather than physical meaning as they recognize that loneliness is as inseparably lashed to ego, as Ahab is lashed to Moby Dick's flank, a decidedly Buddhist thought which brings us to the end with a flourish. The last two poems—Buddhist odes to her daughter telling her to let go of the mind—

> Hush, little one.
> Nothing I tell you
> will ever measure up.
> Nothing else will coax the small fists
> of your brain
> to open this wide.

suggest she has found a spiritual resting place of sorts in Buddhism and the mountains, ponds, and hills surrounding her Vermont home. She sees herself as growing into the world as Bentley in his snowflakes saw the infinite. *Hunting Down the Monk* is a volume of ripe thought from a vigorous mind, strikingly expressed in rich and vibrant language. Who could ask for more?

—Karen Swenson

I.
NOMADS

Come, come, whoever you are
Wanderer, worshipper, lover of leaving—it doesn't matter.
Ours is not a caravan of despair.
Come, even though you have broken your vow a hundred times.
Come. Come again. Come.
—Jalal ud-din Rumi

Hunting Down the Monk

After my father's death, I knock
on my mother's door,
me four feet tall, red leather purse in hand,
fingers soft as bread
and tell her I am headed to a nunnery.
I was going to God
and there was nothing she could do
but take the small nun
in my size six habit, headdress lifted
from the armchair cover,
against the slack
of her belly
and contain me for the night. Even

then I knew a good high, the buzz
of grabbing the tail end
of some god's magnetic pull, like a baby
finally latching onto the nipple for a good hard drag.
That day I was taken from school
I rode to the hospital
in the back of Mrs. Farmer's Chevy
saving my saliva in a Twinkie bag stolen
from a mean girl's lunch,
Mrs. Farmer thinking I was throwing up
from the shock,
me wanting to bathe his skull
in what I knew
was good and warm.

Nineteen, wandering in the Himalayas, at a monastery
in the clouds, I had just drunk the water
from a stream hoping to get sick, sitting
at the feet of a monk
whose skin I groped the night before,
hating myself, didn't I know better,
looking for God in the places
our bodies fed on each
other, instead of the space between. Despite

the teachings, the endless sitting, he was agitated, fumbling
inside his own locked house, setting it
back in order. And again

I was lonely, thinking
of my first love, my first household God,
my father, skull
smashed like a watermelon, seeds lying
on the highway.

How come we aren't told there are no gods, and how
come we still look, knowing
they surface because
we feed them. Shouldn't
there be a name for us, the nomads
who wander from meaning station
to station, the ones
who know better, the ones who
get hooked.

PICKING THE STREETS, KATHMANDU

Told not to, I stalked
the city anyway, hunting down the monk, the incense,
dust, stray dogs, final blast
of sun pressing against me,
pinning me up.

At dusk I saw him
amidst the others,
acres of monks wrapped in burgundy robes
rising and swelling like fire
from the steps of the stupa.
Blue-black shaved heads,
torsos stiff as tulip stalks, bobbing back and forth
from the fulcrum of the hips, chanting
that grainy, lava flow, deep-throated buzz—
exposing the veins I wanted to touch. Jealous,

tired of sitting at the feet of men
whose egos
had dissipated like fog, their smiles
left hanging like clouds
I couldn't grasp. Stopping

by the only store I knew with a mirror,
I vowed to make him love me,
to find some thick and gooey emotion
lurking at the back of his calm, drag it
out with my teeth like a moldy pear. Why

is it we swallow
what we can't digest and still crave
meaning, wasting
our lives picking
the streets for clues, for what barks in the face. All
my life I've wanted to feel
like a stuck pig, knifed
through the gut
with truth. Above the river,

I lay down and thought of home,
caught him curling
around a tree to catch a glimpse. Ashamed,
he twisted his robe back up around his body and disappeared
like smoke.

WEST MEETS EAST MEETS WEST, KATHMANDU

Crouched on a cliff   soaked thigh deep
in someone   else's god   caught
pants down, peeing.

A loudspeaker screams *Jayanti* prayers.
Today's the Buddha's birthday. Rickshaws,
white cows, sandalwood—
women dressed like tropical drinks,
red-robed monks
cling to swaying elephants
like butterflies
to flowers in the wind.

All of us Westerners, hovering
around this   Buddhist base camp,
skulking about like hungry ghosts, mouths agape
craving ritual. We stalk
the natives   feigning nonchalance.
At night, I comb the alleys
for leftover dogma, old wrappers
of former gods. I spin
the prayer wheels, sniff the borders
of other faiths, piss
Jesus when I'm threatened.

Banana lassis at the expat coffee shop, we sit
lamenting the spread
of the Western   Plague,
scoffing at   *nouveau monks*
strutting like peacocks
in their Ray-Bans, Nikes, burgundy hair. I take field notes
on the latest resurrection stories,
tape recorder hidden
in my front shirt pocket:
Anna meditates seven hours a day,
bulimic Lida, tired of Prozac
swears by heavy doses of *vipassana*.
In floats Chelsea   wrist bones stuck out like crows,

bee-sting lips from her acting days. And me,
Christian refugee, religion/science crossbreed,
hanging like a bat in the walls of the bardo,
flying in and out.

Saturday at the White Monastery,
Evan, in ponytail
demonstrates yoga to the baby monks
huddled on the floor, black-eyed,
pock-faced with frostbite from crossing the border at night,
    giggling
at this pale acrobat so   serious,
face straining purple as he flops
this way and that. Next day he leaves
for the Mustang caves. It's what

happens when East
doesn't recognize West's
version of East. West
crawls back into its hole,
meditates on   the void.

Two A.M. I'm lost in the alleys. A monk hovers
like a pesky fly. Tickling my palm,
he says, *I love you.* I turn away, clutching
my pure Buddhism like a lost missionary
fingering the worn spine of her bible. It's what happens

when East and West first meet.
You swat the flies that pester and distract,
protecting your sweet dogma.

Two-thirty a.m. Alone again. Locked
in my room. My thoughts pick
at the lusty monk, his uncouth Buddhism,
I scuttle around the dharma,
scavenging for bits of redemption.

I have this recurring fantasy—
God picks me up
drapes me in His lap like a white root,

cups my head in his palm.

I'm so tired   of moving.

All I want
Is to be humble.

ORPHANAGE, MISSIONARIES OF CHARITY

Praise ugliness. Praise
selfishness, greed. Praise

all that protrudes—
the last red flags
of the living.

Praise this little shop of horrors,
the children who reach
me first, ferociously claiming
one limb
as their own. Praise those

that squirm onto my lap, squeezing
between others, soaking like lizards in the sun
on banks of skin. Praise those

crouched on tables, grooming each other
like apes. Praise the greedy
suck and slurp of gruel
from thirty tin plates. Praise the rocky

spine of the five-year-old,
shoulder blades poked up like a bat,
crouching on her perch
mute, gray, watchful as a gargoyle.

Praise the girl no one will touch,
her body a patchwork of scabies.
Praise the sisters that swim out
to her island with naked hands
to smear her limbs
with heavy cream. Praise for

the boy with worms,
his belly red and bloated as a Madagascar frog's
puffing itself in the heat
of courtship. Praise the one

they call *crazed witch*
for prowess with her claws,
darting from bunk bed to bed
scratching the faces of the sleeping.
Praise the way she flies
onto your back, biting your neck,
her face blossoming with rage.

Praise the scrappy ones with necks of string,
the girl I thought was a boy—
her gender humbly excusing itself
in favor of bone,
the slack skin of her rear
wrinkled like dried fruit.

Praise the tiniest ones sitting in a row
on plastic potties,
spines curved and soft as shrimp,
heads heavy as watermelon. Praise them
crapping yellow ribbons
of rice and curry,
falling off the toilets.

Praise those dangling
over the balcony
onto the streets of Kathmandu—
how intently they focus!
that last moment,
their sharp eyes feeding
on the lives of the living—
squealing as we pry them from the edge.

𝓛EARNING 𝓖ODS

Buddha

Dusk in Kathmandu. The stupa glows
its moon bone. A stray dog, crazy quilt of a thing,
skitters out from the alley.
Three boys, hair blue-black as crows
crawl in and out of a stone Buddha,
swing from its lips, eye sockets
doubling as hideouts.

Clockwise around the stupa,
a red river of Tibetan monks,
nuns, children, goats.
A large woman moves as if sleepwalking,
prayers dripping from her lips,
her body condensing and extending
in a series of prostrations no less
precise and deliberate
than an inchworm working
its way across a leaf.

An old man bargains for meat and tea between prayers.
Two boys laugh as a goat stops the crowd's flow,
steaming pellets
black as coffee beans
trickle from its rear.

A crowd of girls huddles
against the monastery.
Pressing their ears against its walls
the blast of gongs
spread through them in waves.
They scream in delight
and run away.

I wind up the muddy path, dodging gaping holes.
Post-monsoon, the ground swallows itself.

Inside my homestay,
I smell blood sausage. Yak meat
hangs in stiff chandeliers.
Amala lies under the carpet,
her three daughters tucked against
her like mice. She is awake,
checking their heads for lice,
nudging her husband into positions
that clot his drunken snores.

Catching me before I slip by,
she says, tell me a story about where you are from,
and I do, something awkward.
Not till now do I get it right in my mind.

Confession

I come from a tribe of women
ruled by a God, lean and tall,
long, stern face of white stone.
Principles He laid out
like a formal table.

My sisters and I were born
on His white linen tablecloth
our swollen pink bodies
covered with white paste.
And when He touched us
we leaked like toads,
our brown liquids soaking His Sunday best.

At sixteen, we tiptoed around Him,
felt fat and smelly as shrimp, our silly breasts
sometimes escaping our corsets.

Moist and fertile as compost piles,
we worried He could smell us.
On Sundays, we bathed, dried our fetid
crotches, the clean cotton underwear lying
like brides on the chair. Locked in now, safe,

we marched to church, the unclosed parts of us
fresh as pieces of fruit in a Ziploc bag.

Still, my sisters and I
worshipped that Man, loving and fearing
the red-wine smell
of Him leaning close,
so close
His breath scorched us,
His eyebrow hairs
pricking us like the legs
of white spiders.

TWENTY-FIRST CENTURY RELIGIO-TROPIC

> *It's not the strongest of the species that survive or the most intelligent, but the ones most responsive to change.*
> —Charles Darwin

Once, in Bombay, I spotted her leaning
too far out the window, sunning
her Catholic stem
under someone   else's god. Spine
arched, head raised, she

fell over like a potted
geranium crashing
onto the dusty street, parting
a drunken wedding parade raising *Ganesha*, the elephant god.
Of course

she looked a little silly picking
herself up, white girl in hip-hop,
red dreads, tattooed
in Buddha, Krishna, Santideva,
as if she'd been dipped in Walt Disney.   Still, I love her,

twenty-first century religio-tropic leaning
so far East she sometimes burns. I love her religious
Darwinism as she sunbathes on the rocks, scavenging
together bits of God washed up on shore—
tired Islam, a piece of
broken Hindu, a drunken book
of Neo-Confucianism, while Fundamentalism
clings like seaweed to the rocks. I love

her exotic planty-ness,   her
viney-ness, her sticky discontented mood
as she shifts from red to chameleon lime depending
on what branch of God she's on.   I love
her loyalty—still dragging
her childhood God like a worn-out Raggedy
Ann.   Her confusion,

one hand sending up rescue flares, the other
declining the pure white creeds
that lunge past her sure as ocean liners,
matronly, brimming with religious fervor.
I love her

for seeking, again and again.
I love her white neck
bent like a swan, floating East,
defying gravity, nesting
on new species of gods warm
as eggs,

and deep inside, her bright green soul
tight as a bud, slowly opening,
from consonant
to vowel.

CROSSING BORDERS

I. Fiji

In Fiji, *yalo* spirits
leave the body
to tattle on the self,
slippery essences closer to fog
than semen slide into the neighbors'
ears all the juicy details
of a married man's affairs.

What is kept inside the skull
grows like a tumor,
some smell it like a fetid
egg, sense it through an itching
breast, a vague sense of heat.

A woman's secret pregnancy
keeps a whole village from catching
fish, collapses a choir's tune,
nudges the sick closer to death.
Hair falls out, cakes won't rise,
breasts dry up like prunes.

At night *niju* spirits
enter the body
through fluid contours of a dream.
Some possess the victim for days as a dry voice,
illness or heaviness in the limbs,
the whole village crowding inside,
the young ones creeping through the windows
like monkeys,
the elders hedging bets
on what it will take for the *niju*
to leave. The chief, too busy
bargaining with the *niju,*
designates two men
to urinate for him.

II. April, New York—Anorexia Nervosa

In New York, a young girl lies alone
in her room, her bones heaped
like kindling in a pile on her bed.
Too weak to rise
she floats in a haze of light-headedness,
her mind sliding over the day's caloric intake, obsessively,
like a tongue runs over a cavity's
new filling.

At night she lies awake,
her fingers
tracing the terrain of her skin,
her T-shirt absorbing
the night sweats
of a body locked in.

Didn't she read, in Mungari the dead are soaked
in oils and salt,
the skin falling off the bones
like wet leaves from a limb?
The soul resides
in what drips to the cup, the rest
discarded for scrap.

Outside, earth nudges its grubby paws
up through snow,
through the window
she smells hunger, gears shifting,
death grinding back into life.

She obsesses
on the irony of bodies—
98 percent water, condemned to the life of a solid,
the way spring
makes the flesh
a cage.

Her grandmother's hand, lying limp
on the hospital sheets, cold

as just-thawed chicken. That day
the irises in her garden
opened their yellow throats
and she could not help but crawl inside
their luminous caves,
still as icefalls—
she could not help
but eat them.

On the subway
the jarring of the tracks
lulls her. She picks a woman out,
any one will do, exhausted
after all these years, she wants
to be picked up like a mother dog grabs
the slack of her loose-necked pup,
to be folded up,
and slid into the warm,
pink pocket of her body,
sipping at the walls of fat.
She wants to go back,
eyes open in the warm fluid,
lungs soft as petals, bones no
stiffer than cartilage,   before
the shock of sun blasts in
and the waters recede,
revealing the islands
bright and stubborn,
the borders quickly staking their claim.

WHEN THEY CAME IN WITH THE NEW REGIME

they said we were   strangling evolution with our fairy tales,
that we looked like mushrooms
top-heavy with fiction
and need. That it was a narrow bridge to truth and we couldn't
pass over until we
shed our gods,   chubby from too much faith.

So the fruit
of the land was plucked—
ripened gods, saints, angels, holy spirits, buddhas, even the baby
        Jesus
dunked into formaldehyde,
sealed into armies of airtight
jars labeled and lined up
on museum shelves, e.g.:

#21345b
Item: Snakes
Religion: Holy Ghost People
Area of Origin: Southern Appalachia, Alabama
Working Class, White, Rural

#21346b
Item: Angels
Religion: New Age
Culture of Origin: Coastal cities of America
Upper-Middle Class, White

In America, even
the trees were bald, myths
sifted for fact,
churches melted down
for pots, braces, and silverware.

We picked through the stubble—
Christian symbols skinned
to the nub. Beside the roads,
whole bodies of unexpended faith
        oozed like open bottles of toothpaste.

Wasted saints emerged
from fog. When the gods

banged their pots
we were told   not to feed them,
let the hunger dissipate—
in time they'd wither back.
Even the Virgin Mary
was not to be pitied, her cozy manger
sucked of every last crumb. Once we stumbled

across a patch of Muslims
surviving on the carcass
of a thrown-out creed. We had never seen
such savages, rubbing the grease
into their wombs, gnawing at the marrow, black-toothed
witches huddled
around a gleaming pile of bones. When

one of us felt the urge
to pray
we were told this
was the first great sin: *The temptation*

to domesticate reality. We were told:

infinite space, infinite time,

but we   could   not   get our arms
around it. We were told
of Jupiter and Mars—but we vomited
them up, large spheres, soggy
oranges, wholly

undigested. They told us:
sit and rock until the panic subsides.

At night, when we woke, loneliness
in our bellies and we   needed to grip the torso of a god,
they would not let
the spirits congeal, they kept our minds busy,
whispering, *The night sweats will not last.*

The elderly steadied
themselves by the roadside. Some of them
didn't make it, limping
along like burn victims.

Some of them we had to leave behind,
an old Chinese man—
teeth clenched into the Buddha's jade belly,
even as his body went limp.

One bloated nun
by the side of the road, cheeks bulging,
rosary hanging like a limp white tail
from her mouth—
she must have heard them coming,
she must have panicked and choked.

The Priestess Pemavati, Sri Lanka

> Preta: *perpetually hungry ancestors with engorged*
> *bellies and needle-thin throats that prey on the living.*

Even as a young girl
Pemavati's body was open
to *preta*, sliding in and out
so fast she had the whole
village's exorcists
exhausted.

Like other young women who spent
too much time alone,
she grew porous to the Black Prince, *Kalu Kumara*
his long lean tongue
swimming through her,
his heat lodging deep in her groin.
Late at night, you heard her
tossing and moaning
in deep fits of lust.

Each spring, the possessions started up,
each one like a stream gently
nibbling at her toes,
prickling up her calves,
to the base of her spine
hissing like hot coals,
inching up her vertebrae
till her whole body shook,
her skull on fire, crawling with ants and larvae.

One night, after a sloppy beating
from her husband, she collapsed.
In her dreams, the gods came in red silks
sprinkled with topaz.
Huniyan was there in a white turban
and garland of fire, cobras round his waist.

At first the exorcists scoffed—
a woman filled with gods?
Like filling a dog bowl
with honey!

Each evening, Pemavati walks the hot sands alone,
dragging her matted hair, Medusa's hair,
given by the gods for her celibacy.
They started as buds, small
fleshy growths her husband calls "snake hoods."
Now they bump along the hot sands,
getting tangled in her skirts. Once she tried
to break them, and fainted. Now she never touches them,
except to bathe them in sandalwood and lime
or smoke them with incense.

Mary

The fourth time
Mary felt the clot
slide out from between her legs
hot and large as a boiled tomato
she limped into her car
and drove to the first Religious Kwik Stop
off the highway she could find.

At the *Spirit Dancer Gift Shop*
she picked up a brochure.
The next day
she was off to Sri Lanka—
an Empowerment Project with *American Firewalkers*
      International.

A big bus looking like a *preta*
rolled into Kataragama spewing
thirty busty American women,
in T-shirts reading, "Test Your Limits—Find Yourself"

Mary stumbled from the bus,
bleach-white and depressed.

The trip had turned
into a "DWBF"
(Divorced Women's Bitch Festival).
She couldn't deal,
plus she'd burned her feet twice
and still felt like shit.

Today they'd walk the coals,
then go back to the Sheraton
for small group therapy.
Mortified,
she couldn't stand it anymore,
the fat white women
running like scared pigs across the coals
the natives looking on
in hysterics.

Just before it was her turn to find the power,
she hid under the shade
of a lime tree where a crowd of onlookers
giggled furiously, one of them, Pemavati.

Mary and Pemavati

Mary crouched on the ground
and shut her eyes, and began to rock herself
back and forth. Pemavati,
barely five feet tall, stood above her,
a crazed Mother Theresa, a shower
curtain of dreadlocks
falling to the ground.
Pemavati recognized Mary's signs—
the matted hair, the rocking (Kalu Kumara!), the smell of ganja
rising up from the girl.

Moving incense through Mary's hair,
she hissed mantras through the gaps
in her teeth, her brown hands
fluttering fast as wings against the girl's
head as if to keep the smoke from escaping.

Finally, Mary thought, someone real!
She followed Pemavati down the beach
to the small shack she would stay in
eating brown bananas and coconut milk,
rubbing Pemavati's exotic life, rich as cold cream,
into her dry, jaded skin.

After Pemavati walks the coals
Mary bathes her feet in cool water.
At high noon, the beach is a circus for the gods—
men in white diapers
roll across the scalding sand,
others proving faith
by pulling loads of wood from hooks
stuck in their backs.
Pemavati pierced her arms
with seven arrows, her cheeks with three,
a silver cobra
in her mouth, its head jutting fiercely in the air.

Now even her husband is convinced,
treating her like a goddess,
never demanding sex, the bottle given up
for good. From his hut, he watches proudly

as together they comb the beaches for trinkets,
Pemavati with her small knives tied to her waist,
Mary's dreadlocks sticking out
like baby tarantula legs
her body a roadmap of past religious Kwik Stops—
tattoos, tantra, yin yang and Hopi feathers.

Some say Mary is plagued by *preta,*
the way she weeps in the hut at night
after lighting the twenty-one lamps.
But Pemavati says this is good, that Mary's body
is raining
on itself, that if a god entered her now
she would crack with dryness, that maybe tomorrow
she will walk the hot coals.

☙

THE BIRD CAGE

For all Nepali girls sold into prostitution.

Whosoever sneaks out of the smoky hut
long before light has broken
to wash her face in the brook, declining
her mother's offer of *chai* in favor
of braiding and rebraiding her hair
hard as a fossil against her skull,
tight enough for the journey to Kathmandu,
Delhi, and then Bombay,

She shall go to heaven.

Whosoever waits all morning for the man
she met the week before
and crawls on top of his heap
of drugged girls thinking
they are just sleepy from the journey,
thinking they will work in a biscuit factory
in the heart of Bombay, sending rupees home,
watching movie stars all night,
and settles herself among the virgins
as the rickshaw stumbles drunkenly down the road,

She shall go to heaven.

Whosoever shall crawl up through the thick paws
of a cheap drug and find herself
in a Bombay alley, tied to her boss like a goat, tin cans clanging
from her ankles, five goondas
lined up to break her in
until she consents to life in a cage,

She shall go to heaven.

Whosoever has felt her mind wander off and inhabit
the ceiling, watching as her head bangs against the wall
and the bedsprings wheeze,

his vodka burning her face
as he finishes his last round
and snores through the monsoon heat,

She shall go to heaven.

Whosoever shall lie awake
hearing the sitar whining and winding
across the alleys
through her cage
like a serpent in search of prey
until it rests its thin coil
of loneliness inside her,

She shall go to heaven.

Whosoever crawls into the corner
to quietly vomit, wiping her mouth with the tail of her sari,
plugging up the raw spots where her body still opens
to the world,

She shall go to heaven.

You there, Wake up.
Whosoever is in charge of pushing the soul
from one life to another,
of sliding the bolt across the door
once the lame have stumbled in,

Get here,
Now.
Let her in.

BULIMIA RELIGIOSA

On the surface I say a delicate no
thank you to the Jehovah's Witnesses that crawl
like ants around this town
bringing goodies to the door—
the warm pamphlet
with its simple ingredients
only God's words,
the whole truth, no additives
or preservatives. To the Unitarian

Universalists with their
low-cal we're not this or that,
which only leads to harsher
cravings for the real thing,
(Greek Orthodox incense,
sacrificing a big cow),
I say no thank you, I never eat in public.

At night I lie in bed,
anemic, sick of prison gruel and diet-meaning,
thinking of those cheap, creamy answers.

I start to salivate,
I sneak downstairs,
Fuck it, I say, inhaling
their fat truths, soft
pamphlets, and colorful creeds, I cram
two, sometimes three, images of happy multicultural people
hanging peacefully with death
into my mouth till I can
barely breathe. I hippo

up the stairs,
crawl into bed bloated, the blood
leaving my brain
for finer pastures below,
numb for the first time in months,

the thoughts like moths
happily nibbling on Jehovah's
latest issue of *Watch Tower*.

HOLY GHOST PEOPLE

Scrabble Creek, West Virginia

Late at night, in caravans
of beat-up cars
they wind down the mountain,
headlights piercing the fog.

At Massey's they unload,
infants pulled like taffy
from sleep, arms flung in pelts
around their mothers' necks.
Two men slide out rattlesnake boxes
delicate as baked goods,
hold them at arm's length, grinning.

Downstairs the banjo's already started,
the young ones banging the tambourines,
the others singing with numb eyes.
There's Pammie Burgess in the corner
blind, one eye sucked into itself,
cheeks pocked with dime-sized scars.
Her husband kept her locked in the basement—
"with the other vermin,"
he told his friends.
He knew she was messin' around.
He called her sponge face,
till that day in the dark
she felt the Holy Ghost
spread through her warm as wine
and she climbed the stairs
knocked down the door
and kept walking.

In a trance, she whimpers, paws at her head
as if swatting a large bug,
rocking back and forth
on her swollen ankles, nylon knee-highs
cutting into her flesh like twine.

Heat. Greenhouse heat.
Children sag
against their mothers,
mouths hanging in vowels of exhaustion.
Billy Nolan with his hound dog eyes,
doing the two-step right on into the trembling,
his body splashing
across the pews, convulsing under a bench.

Meanwhile Martha Travis
falls onto Jimmy Loter's feet,
rolling like a beached whale
till she hits a pew.
Eyes rolled back, fluttering like white
birds.
Rattlers thrown like worn belts
across the room,
pulled in ribbons from the central box.
Jimbo feels his energy shift its axis,
picks up a rattler, holding it in his raised hands

eyes shut, speaking in tongues while
the diamondback head weaves
through his fingers,
tongue darting into unchartered air.

Everyone loves having Jimbo
back, banned for two years on account
of misuse of the snakes—
a high school boy from Norfolk
called him white trash,
so he locked him in his Chevy with a rattler
till he was good and bitten.
They found the boy huddled in the backseat,
two juicy bites on his hands
his white body gone dry and tight,
the rattler sleeping on the heat of the dashboard,
and Jimbo,
standing at a distance
clapping, watching his very first
cockfight.

Feverish prayers—
covering their faces, crouching
on the ground, some shouting
some bargaining, some confessing,
some suddenly fluttering open
with the Holy Ghost,
then settling back down
like hens regaining their place at the nest.

For the first time, the Reverend's
been bitten,

He wants to fall
down, crawl into the corner to cry.

Mopping the blood from his hand,
sweat from his neck,
he walks through the congregation, preaching

I don't know why they bite, I really don't, I really don't
know why they bite, but if I die
it's God's will, tha'st the truth ladies and gentlemen,
It's God's will just the same.

Billy picks up his guitar,
plays to the ones with the wildest eyes
until well into morning
when they limp out the door
squinting at the light,
the last bits of fear burned off
by the sun.

WHAT THAWS US

Black night, thirty below,
one by one we creep
into church.

We scan the room,
acres of elderly women wearing gardens of pastels,
and then settle underneath the sincerity
of this awkward boy
mumbling from Isaiah
scrawny, hunched like Ichabod Crane, greasy
hair, glasses, pizza-faced.

Inside, stiff-wintered Protestants swell
and melt, cheeks pouching
soft as cake batter. Here, God is soft—
bake sales, crochet, felt letters spell H-O-L-Y.
Even the manger, Downey soft and Charmin white—
baby Jesus in Pampers, God in His bedroom slippers and
    cottonball beard, Mary
with her cadre of dopey kings.

Lights out,
sea of trembling candles,
youth choir painfully out of tune,
Silent Night, Holy Night
and, in German, *Stille Nacht, Heilige Nacht.*

My mother works the stale German
in her mouth, words dry,
then gummy, moist, each one

dragging the sticky past up
    like a child that hates to be bathed, until finally
she spills onto her open bible,
its white wings absorbing
her grief.

Bless her, crawling inside
her past to nest:

At first she only heard my father
mumbling German
through bubbles of blood, his moans
surfacing light as fairies. Finally, his limp spine
draped like a Dali clock on the steering wheel, jaw flapping
like a porch door in the wind.

Bless her
huddled inside this maxipadded
church, thawing.

Bless Lib Higgins
cancer nibbling like a fish at her last sagging
breast, as she leaks, slowly,
into God's porous couch.

Bless them all, these Protestant armies,
weathered minds holding
whole kingdoms
of winter.   Hear

their tectonic plates crack,
         shift and loosen

and the tributaries
        melting into
the carpet,
spongy and forgiving
as moss.

Sleep in heavenly peace.
Candles blown out, lights back on,
daintily, we dry ourselves with Kleenex.
streaming out of the pews amidst canes
and hearing aids, shaking hands mapped with egg-blue veins.
Already they smell of the afterlife,
death close as a meal cooked in another room,
its scent lingering

on their clothes and hair, behind them
the dusty trails of time released,
like tarragon, basil, oregano.

ᴹETAMORPHOSIS

> re-li-gion [*re* back + *ligare* to bind together, to join]

I've seen whole fields
of women sitting numbed
as rotten vegetables. The lucky
ones stay limber, moving on
before the trauma dries
and their vines break off
at the slightest touch. Look

at them in the early
morning, before
the sun even   mentions hope:
groping about, dizzy,
stretching their hunched vertebrae, their knobby fingers
fumbling through drawers of myths,
those pink, soft shells of meaning.

No one loves them
more than I do, the whole tribe
of women, not the dead
but the living—dogged,
blessed, pathetic—
wriggling in and out
of gods like snakes
shed skins.   Come down

to Fayetteville, Arkansas,
where young Julia sits
stiff as an orchid in pressed linen
in the very first pew of her daddy's parish,
his words booming
above like thunder,
her thin neck like a stamen
stretched out. Old enough

to bartend, she drives home,
stalked by a laughing drunk

in an eighteen-wheeler, nudging her car
to and fro, as if herding sheep,
her Dodge finally collapses accordion style
against a tree, her torso
tucked sluggish as a worm
in one of its metal gills. Watch her

emerge from trauma's pupa, sticky, awkward
stretching her stiff limbs. Somehow she crawls out,
landing in the nest
of *Earth First* activists. Now
she calls herself *Butterfly*,
barefoot, an unruly mane
of henna'd-hair, pitted with bits
of bark. Now she tree-sits
on top of a redwood,
one hundred and eighty feet above Stafford, California,
cooking vegan stew on her propane stove,
writing poetry on Ronzoni pasta cartons,
becoming one
with her thick-waisted God.   Pick the butterfly

up: listen to the way Julia
sleeps soundly amidst the peepers, watch
her friend Annie, howling at the moon, reborn
a witch, and Maria, shedding
her stale coat of guilt as she tries
on flowered dresses at Ames, pretending
she's the Virgin Mary.

EMPTY

There is a man you love
and you tell him by the hour.
You think of etching his name
in a tattoo on your ankle.
You think of marriage.
You think what's the use,
he'll die anyway.

You wonder how you'll get through the heat.
You think of how you feel like wind,
the kind that shifts directions suddenly
then fades—
You talk to people.
You eat your food.
You dissipate like fog.

Each night
the moon swings into your empty body,
knocks about the vacant rooms looking for scraps.
You can't sleep because
you want so much, you don't
care what it is, as long
as it's solid, cold rocks
in your mouth maybe, a thick
steel bar you could snake
your limbs around, some deep-gutted
answers you could dig up like potatoes.
You wonder if you weigh less than
milkweed, or a yawn. You don't
know how much longer you can take it,
your chest scarred with tracks
like a runway, the constant
urge to swallow a boulder maybe,
the bowling ball head of a child
anchored in your belly,
limbs sailing like seaweed behind it,
maybe.

THIRTY-ONE, ANTHROPOLOGIST, No Gods Left

If meaning has shape,
then I am searching for a bowl of it.
I am trying to mold the sculpture
of a god,
the firm line of a stern chin.
I am combing this culture
for rock and stone,
the bulges of truth—
the hip bones, shoulders,
and ribs.

Take the one I found
on my last dive down. What culture was it?
A nice Platonic form. I grabbed it,
lodged it like a ship's figurehead
in my jaw. Lugging it home I lay it down
in the living room, the dogs urinating
on the latest quirky stranger. We all want
something for our own.

I sculpt it—
Chalky, Greco-Roman chips fly off,
I chew stray bits like Tums.
Meanwhile, the natives
look at the discarded gods
lying like the faces of Mt. Rushmore on my lawn—
the ones I couldn't get to fit.
They giggle, whisper about the witches
stuck in the coils of my brain.

Thirty-one, no gods left, mouth empty.

I don't know anything anymore
except this:

If Knowledge came to me
in the thickest part of the night,

woke me with a flashlight,
asked me, *What do you know?*
I would say, nothing, nothing at all,
except diving
and loving this world.

II.
NATURE/CULTURE

O World, I cannot hold thee close enough!
—Edna St. Vincent Millay

SNOWFLAKE BENTLEY

*b. 1865, Jericho, Vermont; first man to take photo-
graphs of snowflakes through a microscope.*

Peering into the microscope
he must have felt himself wandering
through the cool, dark
space of a cathedral,
the echoes, the silence,
the sound of steps on stone.
The crystal revealing
its minute architecture of white light,
ornate as an arctic jewel box.

Even in fall, his brain craving
the company of snow,
he crept out in the morning
to study the frost
that webbed the meadows.
And in winter, Snowflake Bentley,
barely five feet tall, stood
outside the church, where the hymns
were blown away by the wind,
his white limbs
stiff and thin as small winter birches,
his cold fingers, his clumsiness,
how he stayed out all day, bent over, blue,
sorting the snowflakes with a feather,
holding his breath
to spare the life of each flake,
the cold finally taking his lungs.

Holding his breath
as he slowly moved
into that speck of ice,
inside the blueprint
of this tiniest of arctic grains—
this dainty white mandala
with its unmistakable logic,

the snow crunching
as his center of gravity slowly shifted,
making room
for the joy of the infinite
opening inside him.

𝒧IMINAL

I. Kathmandu

Listen,
even in   this city
you can feel the dusk coming,
spreading its loneliness everywhere. Someone you lost rises
inside you—
Whatever it is in the violet light,
you know the earth
is shifting its weight,
you feel the sun begin to doubt,
contemplate pulling up stake.
Shadows billow like tropical fish,
you walk around untethered, antsy,
your body the consistency of a dream.

II. Monsoon

No one talks
about the sadness, one
season not quite
giving itself to another.
This is no time
to trust the earth, moody,
lost, the season
passing slowly underneath,
borders broken, filled with loss,
water swelling everywhere.

White Tulip

When I was small, I could not stay
away from flowers. A white tulip
was agony. One large petal
in my mouth, I sucked and sucked,
its silky skin molding
to my tongue, the guilt
rising up and out through my eyes
as if I were nursing on something
I shouldn't:
a communion wafer, a breast long since dry.

After a storm,
lying on the wet hills above our house,
I tried to rub into the earth, wriggle
like a worm into that black, warm glove
of soil. I'm telling you

everything
is hungry, inching
toward something else, who
can stand to be separate from what they love?

I stalk
the earth obsessing
on the physics of density,
the mechanics of spreading flesh
into sky. Right or wrong

I want
my bones kneaded
into that mountain, teeth lodged
in the flesh of that birch.

Even back then I hated
all those thick, tiresome lines where I
stopped and what I wanted began.

Like the bodies
sent down the Ganges,
oiled with primrose, covered in marigolds,
I   want
my body to swell,
borders to loosen,
each pore opening its parched throat
toward water.

HIMALAYAS

Another country
opens   inside you,
as the last light
crashes into the valley.
Blue mountains
rumble with steam,
mangy hills break apart
wild with scent.

A cool breeze passes through,
quiet and humble as a priest.

In its wake,
the need to be forgiven—

the days you weren't pressed
close as a mouth
to this earth.

You drape
your white body
like a web across the hill,
your caged heart dropping
into the soil like a bulb,
only the mind left
light as a cloud of mosquitoes,
hovering over
the warm spot
where the body
once was.

The next day, you record
your greatest accomplishment:
the night mistaking your body
for a field.

A Woman at Night, Queens, N.Y.

The woman lies awake beside him.
Once his eyes shut,
the blackness opens,
fear loosens, spreads itself like pollen.
Taking off her nightgown
she throws it into the rocker. Outside, the streets
are lean and hungry
for anything, the only
light left stretched over the backs
of the cars.

Each night she rises,
leans against the window's cold bone
when something solid forms inside her, pushes up like a mission
to the edge of her throat.

But already
he tosses through
the tail ends of sleep.
Light rises
at the ends of the earth, crackling
and hissing like a first rain.
Soon the yellow fat of the day
will be everywhere, her body
thick as dough,
her mind slow and humid. Soon
her children's gluey fingers
and needy mouths will cling
and she won't remember
the way it feels to swim strong
and hard to the surface
breaking through the filmy skins
that pass as truth,
squinting at the brilliance of things.

At the end of the bed,
the warm dog groans,

the sound outlining the last bits
of silence around her.

WHEN I DIE

When I die,
a large tree trunk
falls on me.
The others go on,
thinking I have cut
through the woods.

I flail about,
grab at the stems of trout lillies, trillium,
my pelvis caught
like a wishbone in the earth.

When death begins
I separate into islands,
limbs drifting off,
the fluid from my veins
winding like snakes over soil,
and in the sun
even this evaporates.

I follow my body into the fields,
give it what it wants:
the last light of day
where everything looks raw
with envy for night.

I lay myself down
in a cold glove of soil,
the bones of my body
stiff as a rocking chair,
my taut skin like an egg,
breaking.

III.
KINSHIP

The unendurable is the beginning of the curve of joy.
—Djuna Barnes

THE FALL OF GOD THE FATHER

*On display, Museum of Natural History, New York,
N.Y., 2050 A.D.*

Remember how I first came upon you,
the feminists cheering as they tied your large marble skull
up in ropes, attached you to the pulley
and lowered you from the throne, like the disposal of a great
    Leninist statue,
and once you fell, the Wiccans cheered,
preferring the gentle cycles
of the moon to your stern white colossus,
the punks crawling into your eye sockets to take a piss,
the Gen X'ers throwing bibles into the fire.

Now look at you—angry fossil, bony archetype, religious
    dinosaur.
Hanging in the museum,
rigged up in your own huge room
like they do whale skeletons and restored Viking ships—
scores of schoolchildren milling by
in their squeaky snowboots,
looking at you like they would a thundercloud.

The crowds called you names—
misogynist, papeist, dualist, capitalist, male-ist, fundamentalist,
    rightist, monotheist.
In the frenzy, everyone forgot we created you ourselves. Even
when your skull had cracked, they kept throwing
eggs and stones. You were so pale.
Your breath still smelling
like a church basement. The crowds
went after the twenty-foot
frown of your forehead while I dragged
your earlobe out from under a Dumpster
whispering, *Hang on, hang on,*
pushing the theologians and historians away.
Remember how I dragged you to the museum,
how they opened the gates as we ran to them,

and I sat there cradling your stiff white earlobe,
as they wiped you down, assessing the damage,
sealing your cuts with their sterile preservation gadgets.

No one, No one should be treated like that. Not even a God.

Now look at you. It's been so long since they dusted you.
And that crack spreading down your neck, your fake white beard
riddled with the pennies the teenagers toss for bets or good luck,
that one Diet Pepsi can the show-off managed to nest
in the fury of your eyebrow.

They tell me that even that old crazy woman from the lower
    Eastside,
(the one with crucifixes glued to her nails)
has moved on to the Dalai Lama. And yes,
that's me in the corner
deep in the matrix of some virtual religion I've rented for the
    night.
I'm at the Last Supper with Jesus,
His sermon was beautiful,
we've been feasting all night.

Still, I'm so thirsty I could die.

I have to tell you I still love you, crotchety colossus,
but I didn't believe in you then. I still don't now.
So don't get hopeful when I take your wheelchair out for a spin
    in the sun.
When I blurt out your name
in the thin parts of sleep,
it's just habit kicking in
when the loneliness gets bad.

Ana Begins, Postpartum

I.

Black night,
   blue sea. I wake and dip,
      wake and dip, surfacing

under the moonglow
   of a hulking TV, alien mother
      of this ward. All night

long she spews her silent colors,
   feeding tubes snaking
      into the side wall.

Tiny bits of panic leap off
   the skillet of my brain

I cannot breathe.
   I need light. Am I liquid or solid?

II.

Two A.M. On the moon, gentle
   gloved mummies come and go,
      dropping off trays of food

readjusting my heart's constellations,
   pressing my uterus for leftover blood.
      Small hours swell and stick

like fat thighs in July. I cannot push through them.
   Me, pale sponge,
      huddled on a stork bed with wheels,

leaking blood and water,
   salt and brine,
      milk, urine, saliva. Meanwhile

a maid handwashes my heart in a stream—
   flopping, twisting, rinsing,
      ringing it out to dry. Ana cries,

startling the pigeons inside my cells.

III.

Her head teeters on its delicate stem—I picture
   an overripe grapefruit plunking to the ground—
      again the maid twists my soggy heart,

rinsing, ringing, and again
   I am weeping.

IV.

Four a.m. Already the moon weans herself
   from her subarctic child. Steam
      gushes from the hospital's gills

into winter's dry throat.
   A woman waddles down the hall,
      a whole planet poised on her tiny frame.

I wake and sleep, wake
   and sleep amid hatching women—
      greasy haired, wet and sore

newborns mopped off and dry,
   wrapped like white pupae
      asleep in plastic basins.

V.

I start to dry out. Lines, borders, edges appear.
   I wake and sleep,
      wake and sleep, latching

and relatching the finicky beast huddled at my breast
   toes small as corn niblets
      ears covered with fiddlehead down.

How quickly she gushed
   from my tight socket, small blue newborn seal,
      steaming on my white dock.

VI.

She's got it now—
   we're safe.
      She sucks and sucks

popping like a cork from my breast,
   smacking her lips, mouth pursed,
      head thrown back with a look of disdain—

she's closed up shop,
   lower lip pouting
      arms thrown back in surrender,

a sudden jerk
   as a dream pulls through.

VII.

She is mine—
   smelling of warm bread dough,
      nursing, nursing, clenched fists
         suddenly splay like starfish, float through space.

We lie on the yellow bed,
   sticky veins of heat between us,
      my bloated body draining into hers,

her belly swelling taut as a milk pod,
   my pudgy cells soft and doe-eyed,
      her lean cells thrashing.

Meanwhile, I hover,
grooming, licking, picking.
Time bloats

and sits content as the moon.
Sliding my nipple from her sagging mouth,
I attempt an escape, she sending me a rigorous

Morse code up through the language of suck—
I—am still here—don't—leave—me

VIII.

Inside all day.

Still nursing, but stormily now, legs kicking,
her free hand batting against my chest
like a small twig against a window.

IX.

Plopped in the garden, she scratches
the black soil, speaking in tongues,
she is fierce, focused.

Clawing the earth
she sits in a daze, cooing, making vowels delicately
as if blowing bubbles.

X.

I know how Early Man must have felt
emerging from the sea,

dopey, bruised sea animal,
soggy with evolution,
dragging wet slurp onto the sand,

seaweed sliding off his calves
as the winds whipped him into dryness.

What joy to experience the first sureness of foot,
truth bone, sediment,
unmistakable ground!

the body shivering into its first dry outline,
a wide smile busting open.

XI.

Dear love, we have arrived
at the beginning, loose and giddy,
we have finally made it, flopping ourselves on the sands
of this long, sunny beach.

THE RAW AND THE SEXED

Lida draws
her limbs into my lap,
her thin body collapsing like a puppet
within my arms.

After a while,
she slowly opens,
subtly reading my body
as she chatters, as if
she is casually touching animal
shapes on a cave's wall
while talking of the weather. She

brushes against my nipples, I
see her cunning,
the way she is contrasting
her raw and my sexed,
preparing for the next stage. I

feign ignorance,
suggesting dinner ideas
as she memorizes
my body's swollen terrain,
locking the swells
of thighs, hips, breasts
deep into the folds of her brain. Stealthily,

she carries them back to her room, plunking
the pieces of woman
on her bony body like a Picasso collage
as she models before the mirror.

Later, she returns, humming,
and again settles on my lap. I don't know how she knows,
but suddenly, like a deer she senses
that I know
what she's up to. Her body tightens,
back straightens,

brown eyes narrow
and dart about the living room.
Faking a yawn,
she slides off my lap
scurries into her room,
the green apples of her buttocks
hard, tight, and haughty.

DAILY BREAD

Long ago my father died,
the death spread
like a storm
through the hills, across faces,
and into my body.

I was young,
I had no choice.
I hadn't learned how
to solidify the body,
stand like wood against the world.

Now I see
death inside the living,
the liquid caged
but pushing and swelling against the skin,
out of the eyes,
through the breath, like mist.

These are the bodies
I try to be near,
the ones that cannot close themselves.

I move close, inhale the breath,
my body loving what it knows,
the past spreading through me.

I know what's mine;
grief draws me
like the smell of baking bread.
It's like going home.

It's what I grew up on.

RITE OF PASSAGE

My mother huddles
at the top of the hill,
shadows, big as whales,
slide across the fields.
The earth opened, the body forked in,
stiff and white in its box.
Standing at the edge, through
her eyes the earth blurs—
she feels herself floating.

Last night she lay down
the tough stem of herself
and gave in,
taking the death into every cell—
each cell opening wider to receive it,
each now soft and heavy as an overripe peach.
Now everywhere the fluid is leaking,
the death inside her, loose and soft as prunes.

Walking up the hill
she pulls the billions of cells
like a galaxy, into action,
the waters leaking into her tight black dress.

This is what the body does
when it accepts
what it fears:
it moves from solid to liquid,
gives in and becomes the world.

ANTHROPOLOGY

Steam

How long we lived,
steeped in those gray winter days
spent in the houses of the concerned—
the wood fires, tender faces,
braided breads and fatty meats.

Leaving the lit houses at dusk,
our feet squeaking on snow,
grief left our moist bodies
like steam.
Like that winter I waitressed
at an all-night seafood restaurant,
and met the night-shift cooks at dawn
as they stepped out
into the thin, cold light
the odor of fish rising from them,
as if they knew nothing else,
as if they were made of nothing else.

The Gift

A long time after my father died
and my mother felt I had become a woman,
she spoke to me as a friend would,
signaling my entrance to a new status
by offering me bits
of secret information:
my father, she said, was really
a lonely man, perhaps
she never understood him.

My mother doesn't know what she's done.
She only sees the bond forged between us,
the past settled like hard earth
at the bottom of my personality,
the truth now piled on top.

She does not know
as she pushes me into the future,
she is pulling up the past
by its roots.
She is leaving holes
everywhere.

Tribes

In some tribes
wealth is measured
by the thickness of a body,
the fattest ones kings of the earth,
the sons and daughters giving their parents
great feasts to fatten them up
for the world they will enter
after death.
It is the duty of the children
to ensure the body's passage
into the afterlife.
Secret foods known to stick to the body,
widen the calves, bulk up the belly
are passed from generation to generation.

My brothers and I
also have secrets in our tribe,
secrets my mother doesn't know,
ones we're not very proud of.
We try and feed her,
but for the wrong reasons—
among us there's never been a shortage of greed.
We see her body moving
toward dust, toward pollen,
so we feed her,
to weight her to this world.

ETHNOGRAPHY OF AN ELDERLY WOMAN IN QUEENS, N.Y.

for Jane Colson

I see you standing there, waving from the doorway,
one-breasted,
one shoulder pulled up tight,
an unbalanced puppet,
a female Quasimodo,
in your pink Nike T-shirt, spandex shorts
the gray tendrils of your home perm
falling into your eyes,
your body a map of bulges and deletions,
all sacrifices you'd made to men before
you wised up:
one missing cheekbone,
one daughter, knocked up
and lying on the floor,
that one plump, misdiagnosed breast,
taken by "the butcher."

Still we giggle.
I empty the contents
of my dog-laden car,
their jumping black bodies
loosening the tightness of your pessimism.

Inside, you sweep, boil water, kill fleas,
change the cat litter, praise Jesus,
and cuss the government,
your ego riding high with purpose.

I sit in your kitchen,
its heat, drawn shades,
smell of cats and Lysol,
the tacky brass Jesus
well-dusted and serene.
You circle around me,
dragging your limp leg behind, fingering

your glow in the dark rosary
telling me the same old stories
of your past
where you always defeat the enemy.

After I leave, you'll bathe yourself
in the blue light
of the TV, sucking on the cough drops
that calm you down.

Before bed you'll tuck the stories away,
placing them carefully
as mothballs
into the fragile fabric
of your pride.
These small white balls
still warm from use,
glowing like moons,
smelling of the death
you promised any man
who messed with you again.

Love Poem to Jane

for Jane Colson (1918–2000)

Jane, they told us you had only
hours to live,
so we piled in the car—since Ana's birth a compost heap
of orange peels, breast pump parts
and soggy teething biscuits.

When we finally arrived,
I plucked Ana from
the car seat, all rosy succulent,
dough-limbed and cooing.

She had been imitating an owl.

Of course it smelled inside the nursing home,
moist and zoo-cage stale,
two old men clustered near the nurses station, wheezing.
Two others lay on cots,
all claw and bone, stiff tendon and vein,
taut neck strings exposed and vulnerable
as the dried roots of overturned trees.
Both stunned, as if expecting another fierce wind.

It was unbearable
carrying Ana down the hallway,
still hoo-hooing, her ringlets bouncing,
exotic eyelashes batting
at those white stalks of death.
I kept wondering if bits
of our sweet life from the car
stuck to our clothes,
like fruit flies cling to a juicy peach,
we were that ripe, that fresh.

No one deserves this much joy.

When we walked into your room, Jane,
my sweet Jane, my love,
slumped in your wheelchair looking drunk,
cheek still bruised, your lungs eerily singing
as your wig slid like mud into one eye.

You were panting fast as a dog,
I didn't know if you would make it, if I could watch this,
you started to babble and bat your hands
motioning for Ana to come sit.

I was afraid she would scream,
shaming your last conscious hours.
So I locked my gaze into hers, saying,
Please don't cry, please don't cry,
then lowering her down, gently, into your bed
of urine and saliva,
the feeding tubes gurgling with plasma,
sprouting thick as weeds.

Frightened, she held onto my gaze
like a child descending by rope
into a well she does not know has a bottom.
You smothering her with your hungry hands,
clumsily rocking her like an ape with a toy,
she struggling to get out.

My whole pseudo-Buddhist life I have known one thing:
life rolls into death,
no stopping and starting, no fences,
no yards, no islands, no birth, *no cessation,*
no eye dhatu, no ear dhatu,
form is emptiness, emptiness also is form.
But together now, you with Ana, this wrestling match
I could not bear, I could not reconcile the suffering.
I could not find a god
to take you in, together.
So I did what I first learned
to do with life and death, when they sit
unbearably close, yet estranged,
I moved forward,

I held you both,
like ice, like butter,
I made you one
by swallowing you
whole.

FLOODLIGHT

for my brothers

The body isn't finicky
when it's growing up.
It's hungry,
it needs to grow.
It takes what scraps are near
to form itself.
That's why you find some adults
with laziness or spite
grown into them—
that's what happened
to be lying around
when the body was making
its upward climb.
Like pitch that hardens into amber,
the psyche traps the insect
that was there at the time.

When we were small
and growing by the minute,
death was in our house.
That's why we're filled with it now.
Not like shrapnel lodged
in our legs or arms,
death wasn't an object
we could take in that way—
it floated, chilly,
so we breathed it in, like air.

Now it's given a room,
a sealed off place
where we fold, label, and stack it,
our minds on it day and night,
our bodies standing puppets.
Some notice the slab of wood behind our eyes,
the sign, *Not home,*
our bodies propped up anyway.

Now we're teeming with death cells,
like a virus, they bloom to life
when the rest of the body is low.
For us to live
is to darken any house,

black, like a floodlight.

WILDFLOWERS

At night,
she gets up to pee,
swimming her way
down the dim hall,
she traces its cool white skin,
as if reading braille,
then ritually kisses her fingers.

During the day
she climbs a ladder,
painting a galaxy
of flowers onto the ceiling.
Post-it Notes remind her
of the correct genus, species—
castilleja miniata, clintonia borealis,
words lighter
than any tongue could manage.

All day long she paints
the warm details
of her mother
into a cathedral
of petals, leaves, Latin and light,
working feverishly,
fearing the memories will cool
before the full spectrum is painted.

She learned young
the body
moves quickly to dust,
that memory has its own
way of evaporating,
that essences are a figment
of a desperate imagination.

Still, she doesn't give in,
looking up to the fresco.
The past must open,

the way stained glass
renews a stale God.

Even now, as the guests
in their itchy mothball
suits sit waiting, she will not climb down.

What she fears
is the past condensing and retarding,
hardening into a caricature
she will refer to as Mother.
Picking it up like a statue from a shelf,
it will come into her hands
cold and formed.

WHAT I WANT

for Robert

More than any other time
I love you most
when you are in the garden,
your body held in bowls of sun,
the slim throats of the iris
stretching toward you,
the heads of peonies bumping into you.
They want you.
We all want to be touched by you.

From the window I watch
your hands skate the soil,
smooth the bumps.
Red, yellow, and blue skins reach.
Listen: You are opening the earth,
the colors popping like parachutes.
My whole body leans from its hungry axis.
I wait my turn.

NIGHT POPPIES

At night,
the thick hands of day
tied back,
the yellow light, the chatter gone,
I watch you
lying on your side,
the broad plane of your back
rising up like a mountain,
your face sunk deep
on the other side.

Against the cool, lean body of night,
there is no argument.
I know what I want.
I open like a poppy
across the small tight hours,
there is no end to my color,
only width, only sky.

If there is a final stop,
a meaning or truth,
I meet it here.
I do not question anything.
I just step off,
the red poppy butting
its head into the world.

POST SCRIPT

for Robert

You can come back now,
I need your help.

I don't know
what to do
when the earth bursts
into flame, the mountain's muscle
flexing with the weight
of the season. So I walk

through November's gray birch, stiff as stilts,
squeaking like caskets. Armies of dried leaves

scuttle along. So many crabs.

The dogs root about. Wild pigs.

A deer freezes, face frantic with scent.

You ask me what I fear?
I've told you,
Anything smacking
of isolation.

You *know* what my heart does when the earth
begins to swell at the seams:

Ecstasy gets trapped
like a bird caught in a room,
bumping stupidly at the panes of glass.

I want to meet you on the other side.

Frantic,
I keep hitting my head.

The Cell

What would you say
if I told you
the goal of evolution
has nothing to do
with crawling out of some sluggish
protean soup,
joyfully flexing your limbs,
buff with newfound solidity,
glistening
with separation.

Or if I told you
progress meant a mass migration
back into the original swamp,
with its slothful DNA,
your white body lying there,
no longer an island,
dissolving as easily as Wonder bread.

What if I told you
my biggest fear
is that one cell of myself
might remain,
my cowardly ego
rushing to that cell
like an army of ants
clinging desperately
to the last dry crumb.

What if,
peering over its edge,
I still felt the full horror
of separation?
What if one cell were big enough
for that old ache
to take up residence,
like some cranky old man
on his porch rocker,

and beneath him,
what if the mad woman
with the matted hair and lightning
in her brain
barred herself in the basement,
loneliness growing like mold
along the walls of her chest.

Or what if
that one remaining cell
were a black hole of sorts,
a condensed ego,
no light or sound escaping.

*

Come here, quickly, press
your ear against my flesh. Hear
the rush, the space, the tiny distant
moans high as sound can get—

this is the sound of loneliness
clinging to that cell,

the sound of loneliness
drowning.

FLYING LEAP

Pulling out the chair
Beneath your mind
And watching you fall upon God
                    —Shams Ud-din Muhammad Hafiz

All day inside the house
hurling herself like a sack of grain
from tantrum to tantrum,
finally I take her hand
warm and tiny as a mouse
and walk across the fields—

I plunk her down.

The pond swells
with endless activity—
galaxies of barking wood frogs,
shad blossoms thick as snow float on its black surface.

Sniffling, still trying to hold a grudge,
she cannot resist dipping her toe
into the quiet
of its cool dark bruise.

Listen to the peepers, I tell her,
look up, our mountain, still snowy in spring,
is a chunk of broken moon,
its chalky chin glowing
like a burning coal at the end of the day.

Up the hills fields of white birch
shred the dusk
with their bony claws—
somehow awe manages to walk like a queen
through the disheveled rooms
of my mother-tired body
lugging yet another taut bulb
of pickled human life.

We head home, Ana now mimicking me as best she can
as I stand frozen in salute
as a fox and her pups skitter like fire
across the open field, fleeing the storm as it bumbles through,
dark-gray whale-clouds bumping and nudging each other,
moving on.

Whatever electricity humans feel on seeing the wild,
the mind, let alone language, cannot contain
but only follow like a clumsy parent
after the child on Christmas morning
as she races through every sleepy
room of the body squealing—Wake up!—
curtains pushed aside, tea set knocked over,
grumpy bodies prodded.

Standing at the edge of the body,
each door flung wide open, delight running in place now,
nowhere else to run,
this is what I'm hoping for our family of four:
to pack our egos like small nervous
animals in a sack by the door,
give them our blessing
then walk straight to the edge
and jump.

NEON BIRCH

for my daughter, Ana Grace

The Prajnaparamita mantra is said in this way:
OM GATE GATE PARAGATE PARASAMGATE BODHI SVAHA
*Gone, Gone Beyond, Completely Beyond, Gone
Beyond Gone*
   —Sutra of the Heart of Transcendent Knowledge

Hush, little one.
Nothing I tell you
will ever measure up.
Nothing else will coax the small fists
of your brain
to open this wide.

In the bright of winter, enter the sun's open
mouth, its brilliant, giddy scream.
Behold the densely packed snow,
all whale-muzzled, crested and tidal wave.

Look up. Even in winter
the wild geese
will still be sewing
their blind stitch of ache
across the sky.

At dusk, enter the silence,
if the past comes lumbering in,
keep walking up the hill to the oldest field of birch,
poised like dinosaurs in their slow walk across time—
only these can take the mind's weight
and deposit it, small, random and inconsequential
as a teacup in the snow.

When the dark crouches at your feet,
watch the sleek pale gloves
of the birch glow neon
pink, neon bone. Behold their tiny branches,

glowing capillaries
inching across
the dark laps of hills.

Nothing I say
will ever feel this good.

Still, even in joy, watch the mind start to fuss,
watch its haggard architects
hunched over their blueprints of meaning, ink
smudged on their face and hands,

I say: let the ink bleed across the page,
let it spill out luxuriously across the meadow.
Remember there is nothing you offer
the fields do not drink, gladly.

Behold the small pond you have become:
this is the first fist, opening.
Lie back, float. Let the slow oars
pull you farther and farther
into this wild and ragged life.

Out there, beyond
the dense coils of worry
beyond the fields we have sewn
so diligently with *self* and *other*,
beyond the swollen landscapes
pitted with language and thought,
go there, don't hesitate.
Whatever it is
that flies hard into the light,
go there, don't be afraid.

$\mathcal{N}$OTES

"Orphanage, Missionaries of Charity"—run by Mother Theresa's Missionaries of Charity in Kathmandu, Nepal. This orphanage serves children with severe malnutrition and tuberculosis. For more information and to make donations contact: akusserow@smcvt.edu

"Crossing Borders"—the specific descriptions on *yalo* and *niju* spirits were taken from Anne Becker's superb ethnography *Body, Self and Society: The View From Fiji* (Philadelphia: University of Pennsylvania Press, 1995).

"American Nomads"—The specific definition of pretas is given by Gananath Obeyesekere in his ethnography *Medusa's Hair: An Essay on Personal Symbols and Religious Experience* (Chicago: University of Chicago Press, 1981). See "Case 4 Pemavati Vitarana" for the entire life history of the priestess Pemavati.

"The Bird Cage"—Thanks to my Social Inequalities class for helping raise money for Maiti Nepal, a home in Kathmandu for young girls who have escaped kidnapping and forced prostitution. More information on Maiti Nepal, as well as ways to help the girls can be found at www.maitinepal.org

"Love Poem to Jane"—"no cessation, no eye dhatu, no ear dhatu, form is emptiness, emptiness also is form" excerpted from the "Sutra of the Heart of Transcendent Knowledge," *Karme Choling Chant Book*, July 1999.

"Flying Leap"—An excerpt from the poem, "Pulling Out the Chair" by Shams ud-din Muhammad Hafiz, translated by Daniel Ladinsky from *I Heard God Laughing: Renderings of Hafiz*. (Oakland: Mobius Press, Oakland, CA, 1996).

"Neon Birch"—This translation of the prajnaparamita mantra from the "Sutra of the Heart of Transcendent Knowledge" was given by Pema Chodron, a Western Tibetan Buddhist nun, while teaching on the Six Paramitas at Karme Choling Buddhist Meditation Center in Barnet, Vermont, in July 1999.

ACKNOWLEDGMENTS

Grateful acknowledgment is given to the editors of the following publications in which these poems, or earlier versions of them, originally appeared:

Anthology of New England Writers: "Night Poppies";

Anthropology and Humanism: "Bird Cage," "The Fall of God the Father," "Holy Ghost People," "Learning Gods," "Thirty-one, Anthropologist, No Gods Left," "What Thaws Us," "When They Came in with the New Regime," "Twenty-first Century Religio-tropic";

Bellingham Review: "The Gift";

California State Quarterly/California State Poetry Society: "A Woman at Night, Queens, N.Y.";

Calliope: "What I Want," "Daily Bread," "When I Die," "The Cell";

Green Mountains Review: "West Meets East Meets West, Kathmandu" "American Nomads";

Greensboro Review: "Anthropology";

The Louisville Review: "Metamorphosis";

Missouri Review (Larry Levis Editor's Prize Issue): "Hunting Down the Monk," "Bulimia Religiosa," "Confession," "Orphanage," "Crossing Borders";

Mudfish: "Empty";

1997 Anthology of Magazine Verse & Yearbook of American Poetry: "What I Want";

Quarterly West: "Himalayas";

Poet Lore: "Rite of Passage";

South Carolina Poetry Review: "Snowflake Bentley";

Sow's Ear Poetry Review: "White Tulip,";

Urban Spaghetti: "Wildflowers," "The Raw and the Sexed."

Thanks especially to Robert Lair for his countless hours of editorial help, to Ana Grace, my brother Karl, my mother Suzanne, and to Dell Hymes and Edie Turner for encouraging me to combine anthropology and poetry. Many, many thanks also to Thom Ward and Steve Huff for their patience and generous help with this book.

Also thanks to Bread Loaf School of English, Vermont Post Graduate Writer's Conference, Harvard University, and St. Michael's College for granting me the various scholarships and fellowships that gave me the time to work on these poems.

ABOUT THE AUTHOR

Adrie Kusserow was born in Underhill Center, Vermont, in 1966. While a freshman at Amherst College, she traveled to Kathmandu, Nepal, and northen India to study Tibetan Buddhism. She went on to study anthropology and psychology at Harvard Divinity School, where she graduated in 1990. She then earned her doctorate in social anthropology from Harvard University. She is currently associate professor of cultural anthropology at St. Michael's College in Vermont and continues to do cross-cultural field work on refugees and the spread of Eastern philosophies to the West. Her poems have been published widely in literary journals, and she has been a finalist for the "Discovery"/*The Nation* award. Adrie Kusserow lives in Underhill Center with her husband Robert Lair, their daughter Ana Grace, her mother Suzanne Kusserow and stepfather Bill Lewis.

BOA EDITIONS, LTD.

THE A. POULIN, JR. NEW POETS OF AMERICA SERIES

Vol. 1 *Cedarhome*
Poems by Barton Sutter
Foreword by W.D. Snodgrass

Vol. 2 *Beast Is a Wolf with Brown Fire*
Poems by Barry Wallenstein
Foreword by M.L. Rosenthal

Vol. 3 *Along the Dark Shore*
Poems by Edward Byrne
Foreword by John Ashbery

Vol. 4 *Anchor Dragging*
Poems by Anthony Piccione
Foreword by Archibald MacLeish

Vol. 5 *Eggs in the Lake*
Poems by Daniela Gioseffi
Foreword by John Logan

Vol. 6 *Moving the House*
Poems by Ingrid Wendt
Foreword by William Stafford

Vol. 7 *Whomp and Moonshiver*
Poems by Thomas Whitbread
Foreword by Richard Wilbur

Vol. 8 *Where We Live*
Poems by Peter Makuck
Foreword by Louis Simpson

Vol. 9 *Rose*
Poems by Li-Young Lee
Foreword by Gerald Stern

Vol. 10 *Genesis*
Poems by Emanuel di Pasquale
Foreword by X.J. Kennedy

Vol. 11 *Borders*
Poems by Mary Crow
Foreword by David Ignatow

Vol. 12 *Awake*
Poems by Dorianne Laux
Foreword by Philip Levine

Vol. 13 *Hurricane Walk*
Poems by Diann Blakely Shoaf
Foreword by William Matthews

Vol. 14 *The Philosopher's Club*
Poems by Kim Addonizio
Foreword by Gerald Stern

Vol. 15 *Bell 8*
Poems by Rick Lyon
Foreword by C. K. Williams

Vol. 16 *Bruise Theory*
Poems by Natalie Kenvin
Foreword by Carolyn Forché

Vol. 17 *Shattering Air*
Poems by David Biespiel
Foreword by Stanley Plumly

Vol. 18 *The Hour Between Dog and Wolf*
Poems by Laure-Anne Bosselaar
Foreword by Charles Simic

Vol. 19 *News of Home*
Poems by Debra Kang Dean
Foreword by Colette Inez

Vol. 20 *Meterology*
Poems by Alpay Ulku
Foreword by Yusef Komunyakaa

Vol. 21 *The Daughters of Discordia*
Poems by Suzanne Owens
Foreword by Denise Duhamel

Vol. 22 *Rare Earths*
Poems by Deena Linett
Foreword by Molly Peacock

Vol. 23 *An Unkindness of Ravens*
Poems by Meg Kearney
Foreword by Donald Hall

Vol. 24 *Hunting Down the Monk*
Poems by Adrie Kusserow
Forewoed by Karen Swenson

COLOPHON

The publication of this book was made possible by the special support of the following individuals:

Debra Audet
Nancy & Alan Cameros
Ron & Susan Dow
Dr. Henry & Beverly French
Dane & Judy Gordon
Suzanne & Gerard Gouvernet
Marge & Don Grinols
Kip & Deb Hale
Robert & Willy Hursh
Peter & Robin Hursh
Dorothy & Henry Hwang
Louise Klinke • Suzanne Kusserow
William Lewis & Suzanne K. Kusserow
Paul & Serena Kusserow
Karl Kusserow & Pari Stave
Archie & Pat Kutz
Tamra Lair & Bruce Edgren
Robert & Petronella Lair
Robert J. Lair • Lois Niland • Boo Poulin
Andrea & Paul Rubery
Deborah Ronnen • Jane Schuster
Sue S. Stewart & Stephen L. Raymond
Dr. Loubert Suddaby
Pat & Michael Wilder

This book was typeset in Sabon and Amazone
with Hoefler Text Ornaments
by Richard Foerster, York Beach, Maine.
Cover design is by Daphne Poulin-Stofer.
The cover photo, "Woman's Work," is by Robert Gorski.
Printing was by McNaughton & Gunn, Saline, Michigan.